Rookie Read-About™ Science

Turtles Take Their Time

By Allan Fowler

Consultants:
Robert L. Hillerich, Ph.D., Bowling Green State University, Bowling Green, Ohio

Mary Nalbandian, Director of Science, Chicago Public Schools, Chicago, Illinois

Fay Robinson, Child Development Specialist

Design by Beth Herman Design Associates

Library of Congress Cataloging-in-Publication Data

Fowler, Allan
Turtles take their time / by Allan Fowler.
p. cm. –(Rookie read-about science)
Summary: A simple description of the physical characteristics and behavior of turtles.
ISBN 0-516-46005-6
1. Turtles–Juvenile literature. [1. Turtles.] I. Title.
II. Series: Fowler, Allan. Rookie read-about science.
QL666.C5F62 1992
597.92–dc20 92-7403
CIP
AC

Printed in China

21 22 23 R 17 16 15 62

What's inside this shell?

It’s a turtle.

Like many turtles, this
turtle can pull its head,
feet, and tail inside
its shell.

That's how turtles hide
when they're frightened.

But a box turtle can also close up the space between the two parts of its shell, like a box.

One part of a turtle's shell covers its back. The other part covers its belly.

Most turtle shells are hard and bony.

Turtles are reptiles —
the same family of animals
that includes snakes,
lizards, and alligators.

Turtles have no teeth —
but their jaws are strong.

You wouldn't put your
fingers near this snapping
turtle's mouth.

Although they lay eggs, turtles don’t sit on them the way birds do.

Instead, they bury their eggs in the ground.

The sun warms the ground and the eggs.

Baby turtles hatch from the eggs.

There are turtles that live on dry land.

Some of them are called tortoises.

There are turtles that live in water.

Sea turtles live in the ocean. Their legs are more like flippers.

Sea turtles crawl ashore
to bury their eggs.

The leatherback is the
biggest turtle of all.
Some leatherbacks grow
to be eight feet long.

Other turtles live both on land and in water — like this painted turtle.

These turtles live in and around ponds, streams, or marshes.

Turtles swim very well.

But on land, most turtles move very slowly because of their wide bodies and short legs.

Turtles have been around
a long time.

There were turtles even
before there were dinosaurs.

And some turtles may live longer than any other animal — as long as 150 years.

No wonder turtles take their time. They have lots of it!

Words You Know

turtles

box turtle

painted turtle

tortoise

sea turtle leatherback

reptiles

snakes

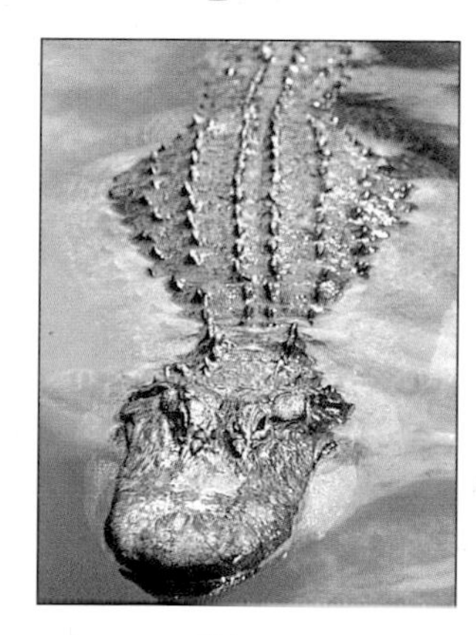

alligators

lizards

shells

eggs

Index

About the Author

Allan Fowler is a free-lance writer with a background in advertising. Born in New York, he lives in Chicago now and enjoys traveling.

Photo Credits

Tom Stack & Associates – ©Jack D. Swenson, 21, 30 (bottom right)

Valan – ©Dennis W. Schmidt, Cover, 22, 30 (top right); ©François Morneau, 3, 31 (bottom right); ©J. A. Wilkinson, 4, 6, 18; ©Jim Merli, 7, 9, 14, 30 (top left), 31 (top left and bottom left); ©John Mitchell, 8; ©Aubrey Lang, 11; ©Wayne Lankinen, 13, 23; ©Jeff Foott, 16, 17, 30 (bottom left); ©R. Berchin, 19; ©Robert C. Simpson, 24; ©Steven J. Krasemann, 25; ©Herman H. Giethoorn, 27; ©Joseph R. Pearce, 28; ©Fred Bruemmer, 31 (top right); ©Kennon Cooke, 31 (top center)

COVER: Painted Turtle with Damselfly